T0394885

COSMOS QUESTIONS
WHERE DO ASTEROIDS COME FROM?

by Clara MacCarald

pogo

Ideas for Parents and Teachers

Pogo Books let children practice reading informational text while introducing them to nonfiction features such as headings, labels, sidebars, maps, and diagrams, as well as a table of contents, glossary, and index.

Carefully leveled text with a strong photo match offers early fluent readers the support they need to succeed.

Before Reading

- "Walk" through the book and point out the various nonfiction features. Ask the student what purpose each feature serves.
- Look at the glossary together. Read and discuss the words.

During Reading

- Have the child read the book independently.
- Invite them to list questions that arise from reading.

After Reading

- Discuss the child's questions. Talk about how they might find answers to those questions.
- Prompt the child to think more. Ask: What have scientists learned about asteroids? Why might they want to learn more?

Pogo Books are published by Jump!
5357 Penn Avenue South
Minneapolis, MN 55419
www.jumplibrary.com

Jump! is a division of FlutterBee Education Group.

Library of Congress Cataloging-in-Publication Data

Names: MacCarald, Clara, 1979- author.
Title: Where do asteroids come from? / by Clara MacCarald.
Description: Minneapolis, MN: Jump!, Inc., [2026]
Series: Cosmos questions | Includes index.
Audience: Ages 7-10
Identifiers: LCCN 2024051419 (print)
LCCN 2024051420 (ebook)
ISBN 9798892138611 (hardcover)
ISBN 9798892138628 (paperback)
ISBN 9798892138635 (ebook)
Subjects: LCSH: Asteroids–Juvenile literature
Classification: LCC QB651 .M33 2026 (print)
LCC QB651 (ebook)
DDC 523.44–dc23/eng/20241129
LC record available at https://lccn.loc.gov/2024051419
LC ebook record available at https://lccn.loc.gov/2024051420

Editor: Alyssa Sorenson
Designer: Emma Almgren-Bersie

Photo Credits: 24K-Production/Shutterstock, cover, 20-21; vencav/Adobe Stock, 1; Francesco Milanese/Adobe Stock, 3; Elena Schweitzer/Adobe Stock, 4; buradaki/iStock, 5 (Mars), 12-13; lanm35/iStock, 5 (asteroid); JPL-Caltech/UCLA/MPS/DLR/IDA/NASA, 6-7 (foreground); wing-wing/Shutterstock, 6-7 (background); Nazarii_Neshcherenskyi/Shutterstock, 8-9; sololos/iStock, 10; Mopic/Adobe Stock, 11; Framalicious/Shutterstock, 14-15; joshimerbin/Shutterstock, 16; dzika_mrowka/iStock, 17; Triff/Shutterstock, 18-19; Dotted Yeti/Shutterstock, 23.

Printed in the United States of America at Corporate Graphics in North Mankato, Minnesota.

TABLE OF CONTENTS

CHAPTER 1

WHAT ARE ASTEROIDS?

asteroid

A rocky object moves through space. It **orbits** the Sun. It is smaller than a planet. It is an asteroid!

Eros

Our **solar system** has millions of asteroids. Some are round. Others are odd shapes. Asteroids have names. Eros, Vesta, and Phaethon are a few. Naming them helps us keep track of them.

Asteroids are many different sizes. Some are only six feet (1.8 meters) in **diameter**. The biggest asteroid is Vesta. It is 329 miles (529 kilometers) in diameter.

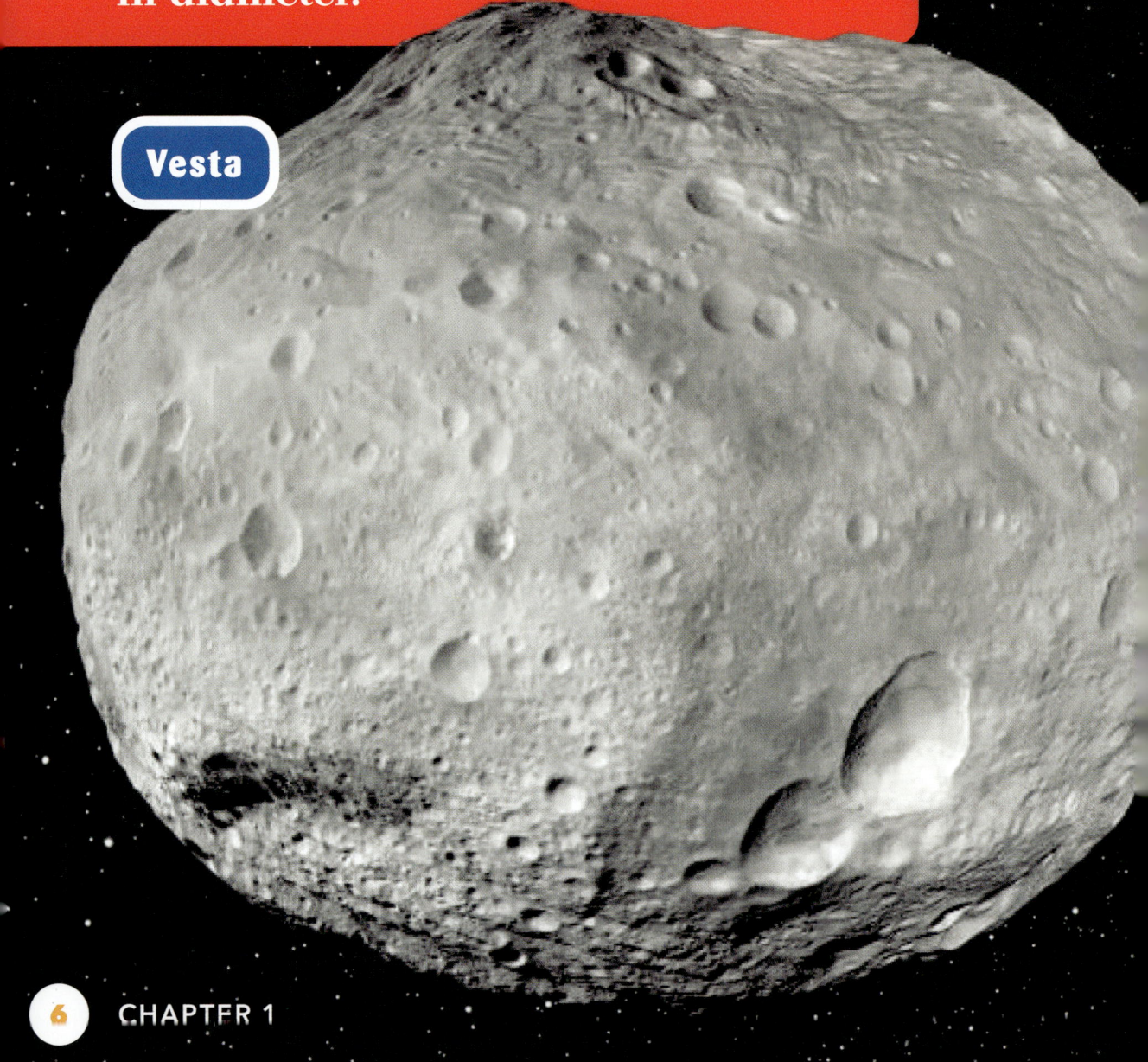

Vesta

TAKE A LOOK!

How do asteroids compare in size to Earth's tallest mountain? Take a look!

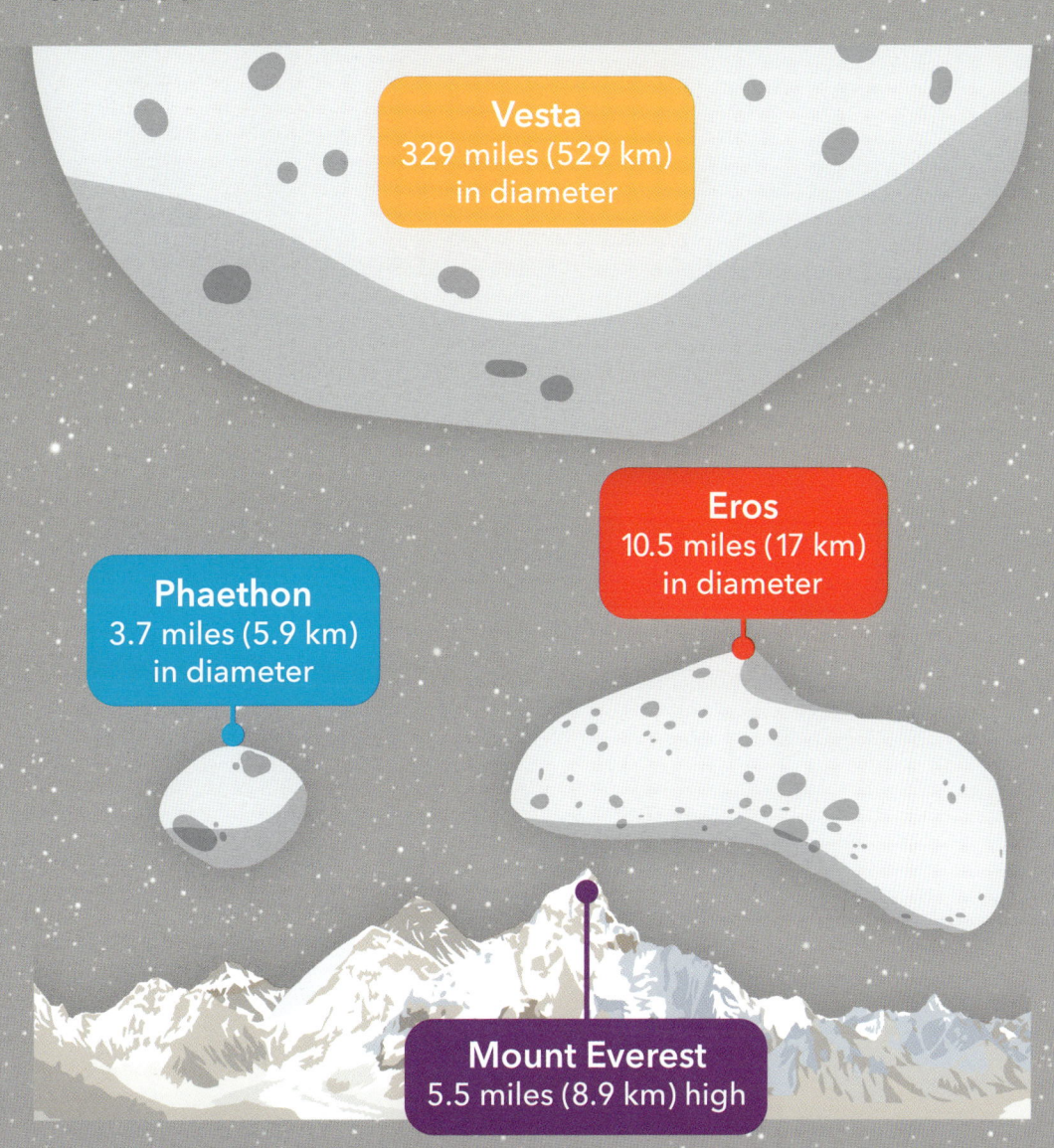

Vesta
329 miles (529 km) in diameter

Eros
10.5 miles (17 km) in diameter

Phaethon
3.7 miles (5.9 km) in diameter

Mount Everest
5.5 miles (8.9 km) high

Asteroids spin. If they spin fast enough, pieces break off. A piece might start orbiting the asteroid. If it does, it becomes a moon! Some asteroids have more than one moon. Where did these flying rocks come from?

moon

CHAPTER 2

HOW DID ASTEROIDS FORM?

Our solar system formed 4.6 billion years ago. How? At first, there was a huge cloud of dust and gas.

It started spinning. Parts of the cloud began sticking together. It made the Sun and planets.

Jupiter

asteroid belt

Mars

Rocks were between Jupiter and Mars. They could have combined to make something larger. But Jupiter stopped this from happening. How? Jupiter is the largest planet. Because it is so large, it has very strong **gravity**. It pulled the rocks in different directions. They hit each other. Pieces broke off. They became asteroids!

Today, most asteroids are in the asteroid belt. This area is between Jupiter and Mars. Jupiter's gravity keeps many asteroids there.

Scientists study what asteroids are made of. They have found water and other materials needed for life on them. Asteroids may have brought these to Earth. How? By crashing into our planet! Some crashes make large **craters**.

DID YOU KNOW?

Scientists use **spacecraft** to study asteroids. How? They fly by asteroids. They collect **data**. They take rock samples, too.

crater

CHAPTER 3

ASTEROID STRIKE!

Not all asteroids stay in the asteroid belt. Why not? Gravity from planets pulls them into new orbits.

Some orbits take asteroids close to Earth. The asteroids orbit Earth for a while. But the Sun's gravity is stronger. It eventually pulls them away.

Sometimes, asteroids get too close. Earth's gravity pulls them toward Earth's surface. They get hot. Most burn up in the air. Ones that crash into Earth are often small. They do not cause much damage.

A large asteroid is not likely to hit Earth. But if one did, it could destroy a city. It could even wipe out life.

DID YOU KNOW?

About 66 million years ago, an asteroid hit Earth. It was between six and nine miles (9.7 and 14 km) wide. Much of life on Earth died. Dinosaurs went **extinct**.

Some asteroids have metals Earth is running out of. We could **mine** asteroids. We could use the metals to make things like car parts and even medicine. How else can we use them? There is still much to learn about asteroids.

DID YOU KNOW?

In 2022, scientists flew a spacecraft into an asteroid. This changed the asteroid's orbit. They could do this if an asteroid gets too close to Earth.

ACTIVITIES & TOOLS

MEASURING ASTEROIDS

Some asteroids are six feet (1.8 m) in diameter. What else is that wide? Find out with this fun activity!

What You Need:

- tape measure
- objects around your classroom or home
- pencil and paper

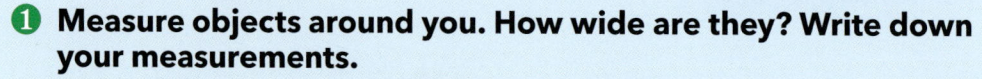

1. Measure objects around you. How wide are they? Write down your measurements.

2. What objects are smaller than a six-foot (1.8-m) wide asteroid? What objects are bigger?

3. Are you surprised by your findings? Why or why not?

GLOSSARY

craters: Large holes in the ground that were made by something crashing into it.

data: Information collected so something can be done with it.

diameter: The distance across an object, passing through its center.

extinct: No longer found alive.

gravity: The force that pulls things toward the center of a space object and keeps them from floating away.

mine: To dig up materials.

orbits: Travels in a circular path around something.

solar system: The Sun, together with its orbiting bodies, as well as asteroids, comets, and meteors.

spacecraft: Vehicles that travel or are used in space.

INDEX

TO LEARN MORE

Finding more information is as easy as 1, 2, 3.

❶ **Go to www.factsurfer.com**

❷ **Enter "asteroids" into the search box.**

❸ **Choose your book to see a list of websites.**

FACT SURFER